100 WAYS TO CALM

100 WAYS TO CALM

SIMPLE ACTIVITIES TO HELP YOU FIND PEACE

ADAMS MEDIA
New York London Toronto Sydney New Delhi

Adams Media
An Imprint of Simon & Schuster, Inc.
57 Littlefield Street
Avon, Massachusetts 02322

First Adams Media hardcover edition January 2021

ADAMS MEDIA and colophon are trademarks of Simon & Schuster.

For information about special discounts for bulk purchases, please contact Simon & Schuster Special Sales at 1-866-506-1949 or business@simonandschuster.com.

The Simon & Schuster Speakers Bureau can bring authors to your live event. For more information or to book an event contact the Simon & Schuster Speakers Bureau at 1-866-248-3049 or visit our website at www.simonspeakers.com.

Interior design and illustrations by Priscilla Yuen

Manufactured in the United States of America

10 9 8 7 6 5 4 3 2 1

Library of Congress Cataloging-in-Publication Data
Names: Adams Media (Firm).
Title: 100 ways to calm.
Description: Avon, Massachusetts: Adams Media, 2021. | Series: 100 ways. | Includes index.
Identifiers: LCCN 2020034714 | ISBN 9781507215159 (hc) | ISBN 9781507215180 (ebook)
Subjects: LCSH: Calmness. | Peace of mind. | Stress management.
Classification: LCC BF575.C35 A25 2021 | DDC 152.4--dc23
LC record available at https://lccn.loc.gov/2020034714

ISBN 978-1-5072-1515-9
ISBN 978-1-5072-1518-0 (ebook)

Many of the designations used by manufacturers and sellers to distinguish their products are claimed as trademarks. Where those designations appear in this book and Simon & Schuster, Inc., was aware of a trademark claim, the designations have been printed with initial capital letters.

This book is intended as general information only, and should not be used to diagnose or treat any health condition. In light of the complex, individual, and specific nature of health problems, this book is not intended to replace professional medical advice. The ideas, procedures, and suggestions in this book are intended to supplement, not replace, the advice of a trained medical professional. Consult your physician before adopting any of the suggestions in this book, as well as about any condition that may require diagnosis or medical attention. The author and publisher disclaim any liability arising directly or indirectly from the use of this book.

Contains material adapted from the following title published by Adams Media, an Imprint of Simon & Schuster, Inc.: *The Book of Calm* by Adams Media, copyright © 2018, ISBN 978-1-5072-1005-5.

CONTENTS

Introduction

Do you find yourself longing for quiet time?
Wish you could hit pause on your busy life?
Feel like you need a break to just catch your breath?

In today's hectic world, a sense of calm can be tough to find. Fortunately, *100 Ways to Calm* is here to help you find tranquility and bring a sense of peace and balance to your life.

Each of the one hundred exercises throughout the book will help you relieve stress and become more peaceful and worry-free. There are mantras you can recite, meditations you can do, and easy suggestions to help you put your life and activities in perspective, including:

Have a cup of tea

Try a simple breathing lesson

Listen to music

Take a bath

These exercises, along with a number of inspiring quotations scattered throughout the book, are sure to help you center yourself and find a sense of peace, serenity, and well-being—no matter what life brings your way.

In a world that can feel overly busy, *100 Ways to Calm* has just what you need to find peace. So take a deep breath and get ready to embrace your sense of calm.

WAYS to CALM

Life should be touched,
not strangled.
You've got to relax,
let it happen at times,
and at others
move forward with it.

RAY BRADBURY,
American author

Practice Walking

Taking a moment to slow down and just focus on walking can be a soothing, meditative activity if you're feeling overwhelmed.

1. Create a clear path, maybe a hallway, or any place in your home where you can walk back and forth.

2. Focus on your posture, straightening your spine from your tailbone to the crown of your head, and standing squarely over your feet and hips.

3. Feel your feet on the floor. Imagine that your feet have never touched or felt the floor, like you're on another planet and have no idea how this "new ground" will feel. Notice every inch of your feet touching the floor or the ground. Be curious about how everything feels under your feet.

4. Lengthen your body up through your spine to the crown of your head. Bring your shoulders down and back to open your heart center. Make sure your chin is slightly tucked.

5. Take small steps, and step lightly and slowly. Smile while you are walking.

Slide the Stress OFF YOUR Shoulders

This breathing exercise helps you let go of the things that are causing you stress, giving you the space and permission to relax and be calm.

1. Bring yourself to a comfortable seated posture on the floor.

2. With your eyes closed, think about who or what is on your shoulders and causing you to feel weighed down.

3. You may have your entire family lined up on your shoulders. Picture all of them there. What else or who else is on your shoulders?

4. Inhale into your belly. Exhale slowly. As you lean to your right, reach your right arm straight out and tilt over until your fingertips touch the floor.

5. Imagine everything and everyone sliding off your shoulders; "listen" joyfully as they scream *Wheeeee!* while soaring down the slide that is your arm. Let them slip right off, trusting that they'll be fine, that they don't need to rest on your shoulders (and that you don't need them to rest there either!).

6. Inhale into your belly. Exhale slowly, and repeat the same motion with your left arm, letting everything and everyone on that side slide off. Give your arm a bit of a shake, as some people will (consciously or unconsciously) hold on really tight, even if everyone (especially you) knows it's best to let them go.

7. You can now fill up with calm and peace.

USE YOUR BREATH TO TAKE A BREAK

Try this breathing pattern for ten breaths:

1. Inhale normally. Exhale normally.
2. Pause. Begin the next breath before you feel desperate for air (meaning, a bigger pause isn't necessarily better).

The beauty of this technique is that it elbows out room for you to rest—to reflect before you make your next move. And that's when you start making decisions that reduce your stress instead of adding to it. Also, no one will notice you're doing it, which means you can practice this breathing anywhere—your desk, the dentist's chair, or even in the midst of a difficult conversation.

GIVE YOURSELF *a* PEP TALK

Positive self-talk can go a long way in calming you down and helping you find peace in stressful situations, like when you have to give a presentation.

If you are nervous about speaking in front of a group of people, try repeating a positive phrase like: "I am calm. I can do this." The words "I am" are some of the most powerful words you can use. Think of these words as putting into motion what it is you choose to create. In this case, you are activating calm by embracing nervousness. See yourself as improving and know, with practice, this fear can and will dissipate. Practice this phrase in front of a mirror and see how this strengthens you. Don't forget to breathe!

BREATHE AWAY *your* ANXIETY

If taking a deep breath is difficult for you,
consider softening your body.

You can do this in a number of places. First relax the muscles in your face, the corners of your mouth, your shoulders, and your upper back. Then sit up tall and relax your shoulder blades. Notice if you pulled down the tops of your shoulders to do this. If you did, try this method of relaxing your shoulders instead: Imagine that your shoulder blades rest on your back like wings. You can activate your wings by squeezing them toward one another (around the back of your heart). Squeeze them together and release a few times. Notice how this gently encourages your shoulders to relax while it simultaneously loosens your jaw.

Movements such as this help you get out of your head and into your body. Remember to focus on your breathing. Try shifting your awareness to the sides of your waist or even your lower back. Release the need to do things perfectly or right.

Create an Exercise Routine

Exercise may be one of the best stress management tools, yet it's often the first thing to go when our schedules get too busy.

Setting up a regular exercise routine—and making exercise a priority—can keep you on track, giving you plenty of opportunity to burn extra tension and stress through physical activity. It's been scientifically proven that exercise helps improve mood. One way it does this is by boosting endorphins (brain chemicals related to mood). You'll be more likely to stick with an exercise routine when you enjoy the activity, so feel free to skip the elliptical in favor of a tai chi class or Pilates if that's your preference.

USE a MUDRA

You may have seen pictures of people meditating with their legs crossed and their hands in a certain position. That's what doing a mudra looks like.

Mudras are hand gestures often used to complement a mantra or meditation practice, and they are powerful means for connecting to a higher consciousness. You can use a mudra to add some extra oomph to your own meditation practice, or use the hand gesture to create a moment of peace during your day. One simple mudra you can try is similar to the "okay" sign: Take your pointer finger and press it against your thumb. This is a universal mudra that represents the universal soul connecting with the individual soul.

Write a Haiku

A haiku is a three-line poem that many people use as a meditation aid. Creating art is a great way to get in touch with your inner self.

1. To write a haiku in English, concentrate on simply capturing a fleeting moment, evoking a beautiful image of the ephemeral quality of life.

2. Here's a good structure to use when you first start writing haiku: five syllables in the first line, seven in the second line, and five in the last line. Read several haiku first, so you can get a sense of their rhythm and tone.

3. It's traditional in Japanese haiku to use a *kireji*, or a "cutting word." This word is used to show juxtaposition between two ideas in the haiku, or to signal the end of one of the images. In English, this is typically done with a punctuation mark, like a dash or period.

4. Share your haiku with family and friends. Post them in your cubicle at work or on your fridge at home. Use them as a focus during your meditation exercises.

SPEND TIME WITH YOUR PET

Studies have shown that owning a pet can reduce stress and provide excellent health benefits.

If you spend just a few minutes petting your dog or cat, your mood goes up, blood pressure goes down, and breathing becomes more relaxed. Having a pet that needs to be walked means you are getting exercise too. A furry companion also offers a way for you to meet new people by going to a dog park. Today, spend some time with your pet. If you don't have one, ask a friend if you can take their dog for a walk or relax with their cat. You can also consider adopting or fostering one from your local animal shelter.

Let Your Problem Float Away

Think of a situation that's
been weighing you down.
Got it?

Now imagine everything about this circumstance—
your boss, your computer, the report you've been working
on for weeks—all encased in a big balloon that you're
holding the string to in your hand.

Now see yourself letting go of the string and watching
the balloon float up and out of sight. If you have trouble letting
go, take an imaginary pair of scissors and cut that
balloon string once and for all.

When you find yourself thinking about this problem
again, remind yourself that you've let it go.

STEAM AWAY STRESS WITH ESSENTIAL OILS

Especially at certain times of year or in climates where the air is dry, steaming with an essential oil is a fast way to get the benefits of the oil. The vapor infused with healing properties rises into the nasal passages, entering your system immediately. Steaming is an effective, easy, and soothing way to explore various essential oils.

1. Have a towel and your essential oil nearby.

2. Get a bowl that is approximately 10 to 12 inches in diameter.

3. Boil enough water to fill the bowl one-half to two-thirds full.

4. Pour the steaming water into the bowl, and then add one drop of the essential oil to the bowl.

5. Lean your head into the flow of the steam, and put the towel over your head to cover your head and the bowl.

6. Inhale deeply through both nostrils, exhale gently through the mouth. Repeat this several times.

7. If one drop of the essential oil wasn't strong enough, or if the scent diminishes, add another drop. It's doubtful you will need more than two drops of the essential oil.

Watch Your
FAVORITE SCENE

If you have some downtime, slide in your favorite DVD or search online for your favorite movie scene, and then sink your body into a comfortable position and let the story take your mind on a lovely side trip.

This might work better if it's a story you already know well, so you won't feel compelled to watch to the end. If you know and love the story, you can pick and choose the specific portion. It might be a certain movie that can sweep you gleefully away, or it could be nature videos—watch whatever will leave you feeling refreshed and pampered. If you're at work and can take a short break, find something on the Internet that you'd love to watch for a few minutes.

Life is a series of spontaneous changes. Don't resist them—that only creates sorrow. Let reality be reality. Let things flow naturally forward in whatever way they like.

LAO TZU,
Chinese philosopher and founder of Taoism

LET GO *of* WHAT KEEPS YOU *from* BEING CALM

This meditation helps you release worry so there's room for you to be calm. Some days you may find that even this meditation doesn't work—your worries just won't go away. That's okay too. Simply accept the worries as they are.

1. Sit up straight on the floor, on a mat or a blanket.

2. Breathe deeply through your nose, or through your mouth if that's not comfortable.

3. Straighten your legs in front of you, and flex your feet by pressing your toes toward your forehead; feel your hamstrings stretch.

4. Lean forward without bending your knees. Come to your edge, that point where the stretch is uncomfortable but just short of painful, and stay for a few minutes.

5. Try closing your eyes. Notice any physical, emotional, or mental experiences you may be having. Each time a thought or emotion surfaces, try to replace it with a breath.

Narrow Your Focus

Narrowing your focus on one thing can help you block out distractions so you can solve an issue or problem, or it can simply bring you back to the here and now if you ever get stuck in your head.

1. Choose one thing to concentrate on. It can be your breathing, the color of your curtains, the smell of a candle, an image in your head, or the sound of rain beating against the windows.

2. Whenever you find your attention wandering, bring it back to your point of concentration. Do this without judgment.

3. Your concentration should be firm but not forced. The more you practice this exercise, the easier it will become.

4. While performing this exercise, breathe deeply and regularly. If this is your point of concentration, time the breathing—one beat in, two beats out—and maintain this pattern. When you're ready to end your practice (either when your timer goes off, or you feel relaxed and ready to get back to your day), you can start slowly expanding your attention to bring in more of your senses.

Get a HOT STONE MASSAGE

If you've never had a hot stone massage, you are in for a one-of-a-kind experience. The stones are used in two different ways during the massage.

Another way the stones are used is
as tools for deep tissue massage. Your massage
therapist will cover the warm, smooth stones in oil
and rub them on your body using long strokes in
the area she is working on. This is an unbelievable
sensation and one that helps wring out the stress
you are carrying in your body.

One way is by providing heat to areas
of the body to make the muscles relax and
increase blood flow to speed up healing. They
are usually placed along the length of the spine or
along the chakra centers of your body. A towel will
be between you and the stones, so don't worry
about being burned.

MEDITATE with the MOUNTAINS

Being in the mountains is a unique experience. The clear air, fresh breezes, sweeping vistas, and abundant foliage all provide nourishment for your soul. A hiking or camping trip, or even a brief day trip into a green natural area, can help boost your inner calm. Visualize being there for this meditation.

1. Lie down outside, if possible; if not, find a comfortable place to lie down inside. You can add small touches to remind you of the mountains, like opening a window to let the breeze in.

2. Close your eyes.

3. Breathe long, slow breaths.

4. Let your entire body surrender into the support of the earth.

5. Feel the coolness of the gentle mountain breeze blow across your face and your body.

6. Stand up slowly, and take a refreshing breath, drawing in the fresh mountain air.

GET IN TOUCH
with Yourself

Whenever you need to calm down,
rest your hand on your stomach or your heart
to draw your focus down, away from your head
and its litany of thoughts, and into your body,
where you are always in the present moment
and where your inner peace resides.

Be Grateful FOR Yourself

Being you means you are able to allow your own thoughts, feelings, and beliefs to emerge with honor and respect. This does not mean you have to act on every little thing.

Notice if you start to compare yourself to others or question your abilities and strengths. Take these doubts as a sign that you may be veering away from your sense of being. Your path is always being shaped by the way you respond to what is happening inside of you. To get back on your course, put your attention on the now, and take time to pause and appreciate all the great things that make you who you are. You can jot them down on a notepad or just list them in your head. Take time to reflect on each item, and thank yourself for being you.

Stop all thoughts. Stop the mind chatter. What you need to maintain sanity is to take a breather. This mindfulness meditation helps you stop and let go so that you're ready to tackle the insanity.

1. Lie down on a yoga mat or a rug. With your legs extended, take a few breaths, inhaling through your nose and exhaling a *Haaaa* out of your mouth.

2. Bring your knees toward your chest, and hug your knees for another few breaths, breathing normally.

3. Let your arms go out to the sides, and have your feet touch the mat with your knees bent. Inhale. As you exhale, bring your knees over to the right, and look to the left. Stay in this position for a few breaths. Then inhale, and exhale as you bring your knees to the other side and look in the opposite direction.

4. Think of your body as a giant kitchen sponge, and visualize yourself wringing out all of your chattering thoughts. Once you are "wrung out," you are ready to absorb quiet and peace.

Give Yourself AN Aromatherapy Massage

Essential oils are mindfulness tools that can enhance mental clarity and relaxation. To be most effective, essential oils should be pure and uncut.

Essential oils need to be diluted in a base carrier before being applied to the skin. A base carrier oil is a pure oil, such as extra-virgin cold-pressed olive oil or sesame oil, that can be used to dilute essential oils. Add drops of the essential oil to the base carrier. A typical recipe is to measure the amount of base oil in milliliters and then divide that number in half to give you the maximum number of drops of essential oil that you will need. First, put a couple of drops of the mixture of base oil and essential oil onto your hands, and rub your hands together to stimulate the scent of the oil. Bring the palms of your hands up to your face, and inhale the scent for several breaths. Then, gently begin to massage the top of your head, at the crown. Next, slowly progress down the body, giving every part of you the attention it deserves.

Use Reiki

Reiki (pronounced ray-key *) is an energy-healing technique based in ancient Tibetan practices.*

Practitioners of Reiki put their hands on or just above the body in order to balance energy by acting as a sort of conduit for life-force energy. Reiki is used to treat physical problems, emotional and psychological issues, and, more positively, as a tool to support and facilitate positive changes. You can do self-treatments with Reiki to help shift your energy, clearing out stress and creating space for calmness. As you place your hands, think of Reiki flowing from the palms into your body, similar to the way in which water runs from a spigot into a basin. While doing self-treatments, imagine your body is the basin that needs filling, and the palms of your hands, facilitating the healing energies, represent the spigot.

STOP and LISTEN

Nature is filled with sounds of peace.

The sound of water trickling outside of your window, birds chirping, or the breeze blowing gently through the trees can soothe your nervous system. Take time to listen and notice these sounds in your daily life. If these peaceful sounds get disrupted, as they sometimes do (by things like leaf blowers or children crying), learn to develop your ability to notice what is near and far. Sure, the leaf blower might be loud and disruptive, but remember the closest sound you have is the sound of your breath. Withdraw (e.g., close the window) from distractions the best you can and return to your breath.

STOP THINKING

The idea of this meditation is "nonthinking": emptying your mind of all the thoughts that sprang to attention and started marching around your brain the minute you woke up.

Take at least a few minutes to simply be still and quiet your mind, and the reassurance, energy, and peace that you need will come.

1. Find a quiet place where you can have some privacy.

2. Sit on the floor or in a chair. You can sit with your legs crossed or straight out in front of you, however is most comfortable for you.

3. Once you are in this position, slowly straighten your spine, raising the crown of your head toward the ceiling and tucking your chin in slightly. Relax your shoulders.

4. Close your eyes or just lower your gaze.

5. Relax your hands onto your knees, palms up.

6. Inhale slowly through your nose, and exhale slowly through your mouth.

7. Spend several minutes doing nothing except focusing on your breath.

8. When you feel centered, calm, and grounded in your being, release and slowly stand. Take this feeling of calm with you through the rest of your day.

BALANCE *in* TREE POSE

The Tree Pose yoga position is perfect physically and psychologically for dealing with daily stresses. It helps develop balance, steadiness, and poise, and helps you feel grounded.

1. Stand with your feet hip-width apart. Feel the four corners of each foot pressing evenly into the floor. (It's great to do this pose outside with bare feet, weather permitting.)

2. Lengthen your spine, lift the crown of your head toward the ceiling (or sky if practicing outside), gently engage your leg muscles, and engage your abdomen by pulling the stomach muscles inward.

3. Bring the sole of your right foot against your supporting leg and open your knee out to the side. (Feel free to touch a chair or counter to help with balance.) Bring your hands together in a prayer position. Look at something that is not moving to help with balance, and focus on your breath until you feel steady.

4. Bring your hands up as though you were extending your branches. While in Tree Pose, think about what tree you resonate with today. Are you a willow tree, swaying back and forth, or are you an oak tree, standing firm and strong? How about a cherry or apple tree?

Peace is always beautiful.

WALT WHITMAN,
American poet

Gather Seashells

*Collecting seashells is very soothing,
and it provides you with a souvenir to remind you
of the peaceful, rejuvenating effect of the ocean.*

Grab a big bucket and go for a long walk on the shore.
You will find many varieties of shells, like iridescent mussel
shells and scallop shells. You might even find some other
treasures: starfish, driftwood, sea glass, and stones that the
waves and sand have polished. You can use the shells
that you find as decoration in your house.

CENTER YOURSELF

The best way to find your inner peace often involves centering yourself. It also allows you to carve out a moment of tranquility in an otherwise hectic day. This is a good exercise to do before more rigorous yoga poses or other physical activity, since it helps to enliven the mind-body connection.

1. Sit in a comfortable, seated position with your legs crossed.

2. Gently place your hands in your lap. Close your eyes. Relax your forehead, eyes, jaw, and tongue.

3. Scan all the way down your body, relaxing each body part as you breathe in and out naturally.

4. After scanning the body, simply watch the breath as it flows in and out. Do this for a few breaths.

5. Begin breathing deeply. Allow the belly, ribs, and chest to expand in three dimensions as you inhale. As you exhale, allow the chest, ribs, and belly to relax.

(The river) knew now
where it was going,
and it said to itself,
'There is no hurry.
We shall get there some day.'

A.A. MILNE,
English author

PUT FRESH FLOWERS in YOUR HOUSE

You can evoke the soothing essence of nature by simply filling a vase with flowers and placing it in any room in the house.

Notice how just the presence of a living thing or the sweet scent of freshly cut blooms can change the energy of the space—and your energy along with it. Choose blooms in your favorite color, or with the most vibrant scent. Selecting your flowers can be a meditative action as well: Take your time to look at the petals of each flower, and take in the different smells.

DO SOME COOKING THERAPY

This mindfulness meditation works best with recipes with lots of ingredients, like stir-fry, but you can use the same instructions for pausing, observing, and appreciating the different elements of whatever food you decide to make.

As you prepare vegetables, for example, make sure that you do it slowly and use all of your senses:

- Look at the colors of the vegetables: the bright orange of the carrots, the green of broccoli, or the white onion.

- Feel the vegetables: the texture, the softness of the silky threads of corn on the cob, the rough skin of carrots, or the bumpy eyes of a potato. When was the last time you really appreciated a vegetable?

- Taste a raw vegetable now and then as you are chopping, and really notice the texture and taste.

- Take a moment to really appreciate and give gratitude to everyone who worked so that the food is available to you: the farmers and workers who harvest the food, the store clerk who sells the food, and to yourself, for making the effort to prepare yourself a meal that will nourish and sustain you.

Watch the Clouds

Cloud watching can be a great way to develop some objectivity on the nature of your thoughts.

Spend five minutes watching the sky—notice what the cloud shapes remind you of, see if you can detect movement or changes in appearance. Just as a massive bank of gray clouds will inevitably clear into blue sky, or a cloud shaped like a rabbit will morph into an ice cream cone, your current thought pattern will also transform.

ENJOY SOME ART

We are subjected every day to thousands, if not millions, of visual images: on billboards, on our cell phones, on websites, and on fliers delivered to our mailbox. Now take a moment to meditate on something truly lovely.

1. Select a piece of art. You can choose a famous piece of art or something you created yourself—just be sure that it's something you consider really lovely, and that brings you joy. Place it (or yourself) where you can see all the details.

2. Focus your attention on the artwork. Take your time looking at its color. Notice how the light around it affects the shade, shadow, and depth of the color.

3. Now close your eyes and see those same details. Take your time to evoke in your mind all that you saw with your eyes opened.

4. Open your eyes to see if the visual image is the same as the mental image. If you notice a difference, do the exercise once more.

Hit Pause

In the midst of a stressful episode, whether at home or at work, we often long for the peaceful moments that a secluded, quiet meditation offers.

But the real world doesn't offer such moments when they're most needed; you have to create them. At these times, a conscious pause can refresh your body and mind just as well as an extended meditation session. Just stop and take action—or no action, as the case may be.

1. If you find yourself particularly stressed, feeling that you've come to the end of your rope, stop. Remind yourself that this is an opportune time for momentary meditation, to refresh and relax your mind.

2. Pause all thoughts and remind yourself that your inner peace prevails at this moment. Think of that peace as a place within you. Straighten your spine as you do this, and lift your chin. Focus your eyes above your head, at the ceiling or wall.

3. Take a conscious breath, slowly and deliberately. Think of your place of peace opening its door as the air fills your lungs. On exhaling, appreciate the moment for allowing you to pause, and then return to the work at hand.

Lots of teas can contribute to a calm feeling: Try something like chamomile or lemon balm. The warmth of the cup and the drink also help you settle down, so feel free to substitute with hot cocoa or another warm beverage.

1. Make use of all of your senses in your teatime meditation. Use your favorite teacup or even your good china.

2. Pour the water into a teapot or directly into your cup. Let it sit for a few minutes. Lean over and smell the scent of the tea. Look at the color of the tea. Is it gold? Think about the color of gold. What does this bring up?

3. Deeply inhale the scent of the tea and bring the cup up to your lips. Before you sip, pause to feel the warmth and breathe it in. Then slowly sip, using your taste buds and sense of smell to focus on the tea. What flavors are present? Can you taste flowers or herbs? If it's not too hot, hold a sip of tea in your mouth for a few seconds and truly savor the subtle flavors.

Take a Time-Out

To give yourself a break and
keep a leash on your frustration and stress,
take this special time-out for yourself.

Lean back against a wall, and press the back of your body
toward the wall. Feel supported by the wall. Focus on your
breath. Try to observe the flow of emotions. See if you can
identify what emotion is present. Breathe into the emotion
to see what is happening right now. Take a few more breaths.
Consider the best way to handle the current problem. When
you come to a place of peace and insight, you can return to the
problem. Trust that you will know what is the best thing to do.
As you come to a place of calm, those around you will feel it
(even if they only feel it on a subconscious level)
and will begin to feel calm as well.

DO SOME GARDENING

There's something gratifying and soothing about taking care of plants, whether you're a master gardener or just trying to keep a houseplant alive.

Take a break from your to-do list today to tend to whatever plants are in your life. Give them some water, clear out the brown leaves, get your fingers in the dirt. It will help you feel grounded and calmer. Digging in the dirt not only evokes the sense of child's play we experienced as kids in the sandbox, it also puts us back in touch—literally—with the earth.

TRY the THREE-PART BREATH

This breathing exercise is called the Three-Part Breath. When done with a focus on long, relaxed exhalations, it's especially good for calming the mind and nervous system. Avoid the Three-Part Breath exercise if you've had recent surgery or injury in your torso or head.

1. Sit comfortably with a long spine.

2. Seal your lips and relax your forehead, jaw, and belly.

3. Begin to take steady, long breaths in and out through your nostrils.

4. Let your breath slow down so much that you can feel your belly, rib cage, then chest expand and contract with each inhalation and exhalation.

5. Take a few minutes to establish a relaxed and even breathing rhythm.

6. Next, begin to slow down and extend your exhalations, allowing them to become longer than your inhalations. To help lengthen your exhalations, gently contract your abdominal muscles as you breathe out.

7. Without straining, draw your belly button back to the spine to create slow-motion exhalations.

8. Gradually build your exhalations to last twice as long as your inhalations. Stay relaxed as you gently contract your abdominal muscles to squeeze the air out of your lungs.

9. Continue for three to five minutes.

Say a Calming Mantra

Not all stress is bad, but sometimes you might carry a bit too much of it.

If you feel panic, bring your awareness to your larger muscle groups (thighs and buttocks) and relax them. Begin to recite this mantra: "Now that I have released all excess stress, I am calm and peaceful." Place your feet flat on the floor while you repeat the mantra. You may even want to rub the tops of your thighs with the palms of your hands, kind of like a massage, while reciting it.

CALL A FRIEND

A great way to find some perspective and a feeling of peace is to call up a trusted friend, with whom you can speak candidly and truthfully, someone who is caring and has a genuine concern for your needs and feelings and has a sense of humor.

It feels so great to be able to laugh at yourself and not take yourself too seriously! A true friend will encourage, accept, and support you, no matter what is happening in your life. We all have a need for authentic friendship, to receive it and to give it as well. Keep these tips in mind when you place your call:

- Make sure you are comfortable, maybe with your feet elevated and a cup of tea within reach.
- Choose to mindfully talk with your friend, asking for her support during a stressful time, mindfully connecting with someone who understands and cares about you.

You know that listening to music can lift your mood, give you energy, or take your edge off. You may not know that it can also be a health tonic—researchers have found a wide range of health benefits that result from listening to music, including altered perceptions of pain. Music also triggers the release of endorphins.

Today, devote your full attention to a piece of music you love. You can do this during your commute, as you do the dishes, or as part of a wind-down routine before bed. Bonus points for singing along, as singing has been shown to reduce cortisol, a stress-related hormone.

BE LATE FOR WORK

Call or email your boss this morning and say you'll be a little late. Use that bit of extra time to do something nice for yourself.

Make a delicious breakfast, do some yoga, have sex, or take the dog for a longer walk. Sometimes it can seem like we're always rushing around, so this morning take all the time you need. You won't be stuck in traffic on your way to work, and chances are you'll have a much more pleasant, less stressful day.

Imagine a Meadow

This meditation walks you through a peaceful, calming visual.

1. Lie down if possible; if not, sit comfortably.

2. Imagine you are lying in the middle of a mountain meadow filled with wildflowers. Smell the earth, the fragrant flowers, and the wild grasses.

3. Imagine that a mountain stream is off in the distance.

4. Imagine all of your concerns, worries, hurts, and disappointments floating away.

5. Relax, and let go of all thought.

6. When you feel calm at your center, stand up slowly and take a short walk in your surroundings, reveling in the beauty around you.

When instead of reacting against a situation, you merge with it, the solution arises out of the situation itself.

ECKHART TOLLE,
German-born spiritual teacher and author

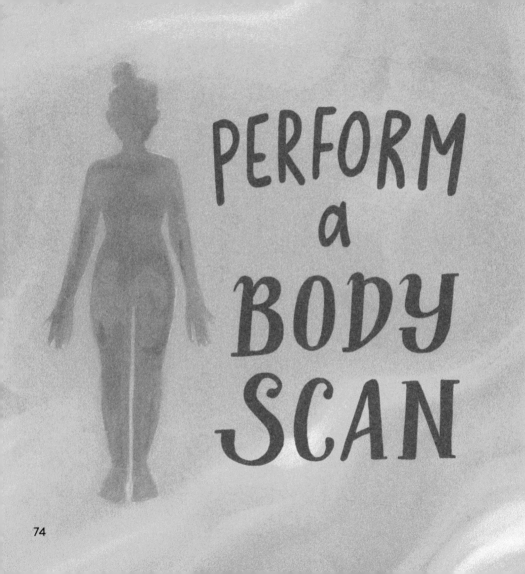

PERFORM a BODY SCAN

An important way to bring yourself into the present moment, and to release any stress or tension you're carrying in your body, is to do a body scan.

1. Lie on your back, with your legs outstretched comfortably on the floor. Place a pillow or cushion underneath your knees.

2. Take a slow, deep inhale through your nose and exhale through your mouth. Let go. Feel yourself supported by the ground, by the earth.

3. Then turn your attention to your right foot. Notice your toes; relax the entire foot. Relax the right ankle. Feel your entire right leg. Relax the right leg. Notice the right side of your torso. Relax the right side of your torso. Relax the right shoulder. Relax the top of the right arm. Relax the forearm. Relax the right hand, including the right fingers. Now do the same for your left foot.

4. Relax the lower back. Relax the middle of your back. Relax the shoulder blades. Relax the neck. Relax the jaw. Relax the tongue. Relax the eyelids. Relax the temples. Relax the brow. Relax the entire head.

Release YOUR TENSION

If you're still wired at the end of your day, you can try tense-and-release exercises to calm down.

1. Tense or curl your toes under, inhale, and then relax your toes as you exhale.

2. Tense your feet by pretending you are pointing your toes toward your forehead and pushing your heels away. Inhale while they are tense, and as you exhale, relax your feet.

3. Tense or squeeze your bottom and your entire legs, feet, and toes at the same time. Inhale, and as you exhale, release your bottom, legs, feet, and toes.

4. Pull your stomach in tight, until your rib cage is sticking out; bring your shoulders up to your ears. Inhale, and as you exhale, relax your tummy and your shoulders.

5. Clench your arms and your hands (making a tight fist), lifting them about 1 or 2 inches off the bed. Inhale, and as you exhale, relax your arms and hands, dropping them back on the bed.

6. Close your eyes really tight, and close your mouth really tight. Inhale, and as you exhale, relax your face.

7. Clench your entire body, including your bottom and face, and inhale. Hold this for a few seconds, and then, as you exhale, say a long *ahhhhhhhh*.

DO a FORWARD FOLD

If your day is not going well, and you need a time-out to calm down, try this exercise.

1. Stand with your feet hip-width apart, with toes facing forward. Bring your arms to your sides.

2. Allow your tailbone to reach downward, and lengthen your spine upward. Press out through the crown of your head. Soften your knees so they are slightly bent.

3. Reach your arms up above your head, inhale, and as you exhale, fold over to touch your toes or reach close to them.

4. Stay for a few breaths. Gently nod yes, then gently shake your head no.

5. Come up slowly, rolling one vertebra over the other. Your head should come up last.

Recite a Shield Mantra

This visualization is a powerful energetic defense against stress and negative energy.

1   Repeat the mantra: "I am protected by the golden light that surrounds me now."

2   Visualize bad energy bouncing off your light and away, and your bright light shining against the darkness of a bad mood.

Take
A
Bath

Turn off your overhead lights and light a few candles. Add fragrant bath oil or bath salts to the water, and play soft, soothing music, if you like.

1   Once you're in the water, take a few deep breaths and exhale.

2   Imagine the water washing away the stresses of the moment so you can emerge feeling refreshed and rested.

3   Say a prayer of gratitude for the bath and for the clean water. Bring your palms together, and lower them to your chest (home of the heart chakra), pressing your thumbs into your heart center in a final prayer of gratitude.

4   Before you end your bath, close your eyes, and smell the scent of the soap or oil you are using. Listen to the water as you slowly move around.

5   When you are ready, step out slowly and gently, and wrap yourself in a soft, dry towel. Slather lotion on your arms and legs and everywhere you want to retain moisture.

6   Before you slip into your pajamas, lift your arms up and over your head, gently arching your back while you enjoy a few more *ahhhhh* breaths. Enjoy the feeling of being relaxed, scented, and rejuvenated.

GROUND

Picture in your mind a large, old tree.
See its strong root system and flexible branches.
You also have a strong root system, capable of
providing security and peace.

YOURSELF

Repeat this mantra:
"Being firmly grounded into my body offers me peace."

When using this mantra, soften your solar plexus,
and when you exhale, imagine directing your
energy out through your legs into the ground.

Feel YOUR Breath

Sit (or lie down), rest your hand on your belly, and feel your breath. As you breathe in, your belly will rise, and as you breathe out, it will fall.

Follow your breath for a while. Then start to breathe at this rhythm: Count to five on the inhale, and count to five on the exhale. Breathe however is most comfortable for you. If you want to make this exercise even more powerful, you can breathe in through your nose and out through your mouth. If you'd like, make the exhale audible with an *ahh*. Do this for a few minutes, and notice how the simple act of breathing can calm your emotions.

Light Some Incense

Incense imparts a feeling of the sacred and can support the atmosphere of meditation. Here are some suggestions for incense selections:

- For facilitating breath work: Eucalyptus, pine, and lavender are clean and penetrating scents.

- For mental focus: Basil, geranium, and frankincense penetrate deeply through the emotional sphere and have lasting power.

- For purifying emotions: Jasmine, vetiver, sage, and cypress have a calming effect on mood.

- For neutralizing stress: Rosemary reduces melancholy, and scents of the mint family (peppermint, spearmint) are mentally uplifting.

- For an inspirational atmosphere: Patchouli, sandalwood, and myrrh are the traditional ingredients for liturgical incense.

How can one ever know anything if they are too busy thinking?

GAUTAMA BUDDHA,
Indian spiritual leader and
founder of Buddhism

Go Enjoy Nature

Doing a walking meditation outdoors is a great way to get in touch with your inner calm and draw peaceful energy from the world around you, especially the green spaces that connect us with the calming energy of nature.

1. Choose a place for a quiet walk in nature—a nature path, a park, a tree-lined part of your neighborhood, or even your own garden. All of these will work, as long as you can see nature and feel natural energy.

2. Tread softly. Open your heart. Take a moment to be grateful for all of the blessings of everything that is good and beautiful in each moment and in each step that you take.

3. Notice the peace in your environment, and how nature reaches out to connect different things, like new vines creeping across old dead trees, or how green shoots grow between the cracks in the sidewalk.

4. Maintain a calm awareness of your body and your feelings as you walk.

5. As peace wraps around you, reach out to send calm from your heart to others with the knowledge that your thoughts, intentions, and emotions are carrying a feeling of peace to whomever you choose to receive it.

MAKE A CALMING VISION BOARD

You can use pictures of your friends, family, and your partner, as well as special memories, trips, and vacations, and combine them with pictures you pull from magazines or your favorite websites to create a calming collage.

Create your own story. Make this activity mindful by reflecting on what the art says about where your heart is. If the collage shows things that you aspire to have or be, consider why you're not making them part of your life now. By taking the time to consider your past, what you love now, and where you dream of going in the future, you can stop obsessing over the daily stresses in the here and now and remember that you are blessed.

Cup Your Eyes

Here's a quick yet surprisingly effective meditation that can be done anywhere when you need to regroup and calm down.

1. Cup your hands over your eyes, enough so that you cannot see any light. Close your eyes and feel the darkness for a few slow breaths.

2. While your hands are still cupped over your eyes, open your eyes slowly. This may feel very peaceful. Imagine that you are in the deep shade, in the middle of a forest. Invite peace into your little "cupped" space.

3. When you feel peace entering and feel reassured that you are ready to handle whatever comes, remove your hands.

Chop
YOUR WAY TO
Calm

When you're feeling particularly stressed, you can often feel it in your gut. This is because the body holds many emotions and stresses between the belly button and the rib cage (the third chakra, or solar plexus chakra).

1. Take a minute to warm up your core: Jog in place, walk around your room, or do a few jumping jacks to loosen up. Once you're finished, stand with your feet aligned with your shoulders at a distance of about a foot apart. Slightly bend your knees.

2. Press your palms together and raise your arms over your head. Think of your arms and hands working together as a big chef's knife, ready to smash down on a watermelon.

3. Exclaim *Ha!* (the sound associated with the third chakra) loudly as you heave down your arms and hands in a single, swift movement to release emotional energy. Repeat until you feel emptied and calm.

4. Move your mat to the wall. Lie on your back with your legs up the wall, with your arms out to either side and palms open, and eyes closed.

5. Breathe away any remaining stress until you settle down and feel at peace.

LOOK for the LIGHT AROUND YOU

You may have heard the word namaste *at your yoga class or seen it on a T-shirt. The translation for this Sanskrit phrase of greeting is something like "I bow to the Divine in you" or "The light in me sees the light in you."*

This phrase acknowledges that the world is made of goodness and light. It's important to remember this, especially when you are feeling anxious, stressed, or worried. You can recognize and take comfort in the light and energy that come from the people and things that are all around you. Saying *namaste* in greeting is a gentle way to bless the world and all its beings.

Be Here, Right Now

If you are feeling scattered or overwhelmed, reminding yourself to be present can help center you. True inner peace happens when you connect to the present moment.

You can remind yourself with a simple mantra: "Be here, right now." Before reciting this mantra, firmly plant your two feet on the ground. Picture them as roots of a tree anchoring into the earth. Now exhale into the core of your essence, drawing your belly button in, and whisper to yourself, "Be here, right now." You can also add:

"Peace. Peace. Peace."

No need to hurry.
No need to sparkle.
No need to be anybody
but oneself.

VIRGINIA WOOLF,
English author

Do an Object Meditation

Find an object that is beautiful or interesting to you.

1. Keep your eyes focused on the object without looking away.

2. Begin to breathe deeply.

3. Keep your every thought and all awareness on the physical aspects of the object.

4. Once you feel calm and focused, close your eyes and concentrate on the object. Stay with this meditation for at least five minutes.

CHILL OUT WITH THE MOON

This breathing pattern is called Lunar Breath. If you suffer from low blood pressure, colds, flu, or any other respiratory conditions, avoid this breath exercise.

1. Sit comfortably with a long spine.

2. Hold up your right hand and fold your index and middle fingers into the palm of your hand, keeping the thumb, ring finger, and pinky extended.

3. Seal your right nostril with your thumb and take a slow and complete breath in through your left nostril.

4. Seal your left nostril with your ring finger, release your thumb, and exhale out of the right nostril.

5. Repeat this sequence—inhaling through your left nostril and exhaling through your right.

6. Continue for three to five minutes.

Try a Simple Breathing Lesson

Breathing is not something most people are taught how to do, but luckily you do not have to be formally trained to learn how to breathe well. You can start right now by reciting this mantra.

Take a long, slow, deep inhale (inflating your lower belly) and a slow, extended exhale (drawing your navel in), and recite this soothing phrase between each breath:

"My breath is deep; my eyes are soft; I am at peace."

Do this for five rounds.

SCAN your CHAKRAS

Here's an exercise to bring your focus to all your chakras (the places of energy in your body).

 Start at the root chakra, centered at the base of your spine. This chakra is about stability and grounding. Imagine it glowing bright red.

2. Next, visualize your sacral chakra, about 3 inches below your belly button. This is the chakra of emotions. Imagine a bright orange color.

3. Bring your attention to the solar plexus chakra, right at your diaphragm or upper belly. This chakra is about your inner strength and self-esteem. Imagine it with a bright yellow glow.

4. Move to your heart chakra, at the center of your chest about the height of your heart. This chakra is about love and compassion. Imagine a vibrant emerald green glowing from it.

5. Focus on your throat chakra, at the base of your neck. This chakra is about communicating. Visualize it glowing blue.

6. Bring your attention to your third eye chakra, at the center of your forehead. This is the chakra of insight, and it glows purple or indigo.

7. Finally, place your hands on top of your head at the crown chakra. Through your hands, visualize healing white light flooding your brain. Feel yourself relax.

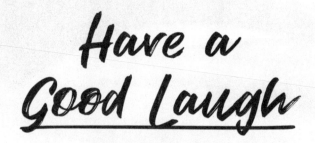

Have a Good Laugh

Laughter is like medicine.
It breaks up negativity, and calms your
fears and anxieties.

The laughing sounds of *ha* and *he* increase the movement of energy in your body. If you feel stressed or worried, take some time to watch your favorite funny movie or comedy special, a classic cartoon, or read through your favorite web comic. You can even search for funny Internet videos; there are hours of content compiled to make you giggle. Once you get a good belly laugh going, close your eyes and embrace that feeling of laughing very hard, deep in your belly. The power and positive energy of a good laugh can soothe negative emotions, and help you calm yourself down even after a very tough day.

Adopt the pace of nature:
her secret is patience.

RALPH WALDO EMERSON,
American poet and author

Meditate On Water

This is a great meditation to do if you get a chance to spend time by a body of water.

Walk around and see if you can feel watery. Move as if you had no bones. Feel fluid. Close your eyes. Consider the healing properties of water, just in the functions of your body:

- Rivers of tears, sometimes pouring out of you, and at other times just a trickle.
- The motion of your cells, the movement of your thoughts and feelings zipping around your brain—all the systems of your body are flowing.

You, too, are always flowing and changing. You can let the things that are bothering you flow away from you right now.

SHOUT IT OUT

Being calm and mindful doesn't mean you won't ever get angry or upset again. But it can help you express those emotions in a more conscious way.

If you've got some anger to express, let it out with a primal scream (preferably somewhere solitary where you won't scare anyone else, like in the car). Do it with the intention of getting the feelings out of your body and into the air where they can dissipate. This exercise gives your frustrations a voice.

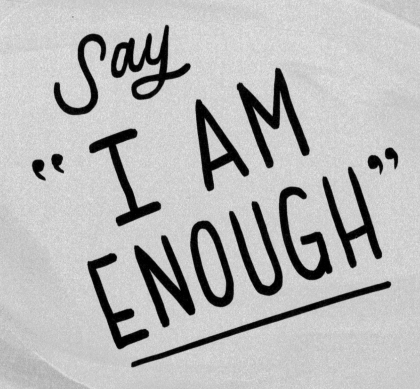

Very often, new beginnings can be tough. For example, you might start a new business and then suddenly fear you don't have enough experience. Or maybe you are a new mother and suddenly feel overwhelmed by the responsibility.

In times like these, remind yourself that you are whole, and you are good enough exactly as you are. Take a moment and breathe in through your nose and out through your mouth. Connect to your heart and state out loud: "I am enough."

Do DOWNWARD

Because it stretches your entire back, strengthens your upper body, and improves circulation—all in a minute or less—the Downward Facing Dog yoga pose is a perfect way to refresh yourself and fight physical and mental stress.

1. To do the pose, start on your hands and knees.
2. Tuck your toes under, then straighten your legs and lift your hips up so you make the shape of an upside down V.

FACING DOG

3 Press strongly into your palms to move more of your weight back toward your heels, which are reaching down to the floor. Let your head dangle.

4 To make the pose more relaxing, rest your forehead (right at the hairline) on a stack of books or a yoga block. To make it more energizing, come forward into the top of a push-up position, or Plank Pose, as you inhale and move back into Downward Dog with each exhalation for a total of five cycles.

VISUALIZE A LAKE

Sometimes you can quiet your body, but your thoughts dance on. Let them. Here is a meditation to help you follow your thoughts rather than fight them.

1. Choose a comfortable sitting position.

2. Straighten your spine. Rest your hands, palm up, on your thighs.

3. Close your eyes. Take a couple of cleansing breaths and then breathe in and out in a slow rhythm. Relax. Mentally let go of thoughts about your external environment. Let your heart be open and receptive.

4. Imagine your mind is a lake. Your restless thoughts are ripples pushed by a breeze blowing across the surface.

Even the tallest trees are able to grow from tiny seeds like these. Remember this, and try not to rush time.

PAULO COELHO,
Brazilian lyricist and author

SAY a CHANT for COMPASSION

Pronounced as it is spelled, Om Mani Padme Hum,
one of the most popular mantras in the world,
is intended to create compassion.

Many people will begin saying it and transition into singing it, formulating their own tune. Roughly translated, it means, "When the heart and the mind get together and combine efforts, then anything is possible." So whenever you need some mantra mojo, try saying, then chanting (or singing): Om Mani Padme Hum...Om Mani Padme Hum.

A yoga concept called *Naad* holds that the roof of your mouth has eighty-four meridian points (located along energy channels) that can be stimulated when your tongue strikes them, such as when speaking. According to *Naad*, the meridian points stimulate the brain's hypothalamus, which stimulates the pineal gland, which stimulates the pituitary gland. The pituitary gland and the entire glandular system play a role in experiencing emotions and achieving bliss; this connection means that the sound of a word (and the meridian the tongue strikes while saying the word) is just as important as what the word means. Over thousands of years, yogis have created mantras designed to strike meridians that will facilitate a meditative state. Om Mani Padme Hum!

Breathe
LIKE A
Lion

The Lion's Breath breathing exercise in yoga stimulates the nerves, senses, and mind, and energizes the immune system. It's also amazingly refreshing and helpful for letting go of stress. Avoid this breath if you have recent or chronic injury to the knees, face, neck, or tongue.

1. Sit in a comfortable position. Ground your weight down into your bottom and reach the crown of the head up to lengthen the spine. Take a moment to relax your body.

2. Close your mouth and notice your breath flowing in and out of your nostrils. Allow it to become steady and rhythmic.

3. Place your hands on your thighs with your fingers fanned out.

4. Inhale deeply through your nose as you draw your belly inward and press your chest forward, arching your upper back. Lift your chin, open your eyes wide, and gaze upward at the spot between the eyebrows.

5. Open your mouth and stick out your tongue. Stretch the tip of your tongue down toward the chin, and slowly exhale all of the breath out, while whispering a loud, strong *Haaaa* sound.

6. Repeat steps 4 and 5 four to six times. Then pause and relax.

ENJOY A TENNIS BALL MASSAGE

1. Lie down on your yoga mat.

2. Place a used tennis ball under your back, between your spine and your left shoulder blade.

3. Bend your left knee, placing your foot up close to your bottom.

4. Inhale, and release your hands down by your sides.

5. Exhale, and let the weight of your body slowly come down onto the tennis ball.

6. Press into your left foot to roll your back a few inches up and down over the ball.

7. Find your most tender knot, and allow your body to sink over the ball. Say (or moan) *Ohhhhh*.

Hand-Wash Your Dishes

Doing chores mindfully can be a sort of meditation, especially after a long day. It can feel good to focus fully on a manual task, especially one that benefits you and your household.

Washing dishes is a perfect example of a chore that can be done mindfully. Fill the sink with soapy water (try to be a mindful shopper and buy products that are beautifully scented and perhaps organic). When you plunge your hands into the soapy water, enjoy the sensation of warmth. Then wash each glass and dish slowly, surrendering any desire to rush the process or to focus on getting them all done. Rather, focus on just one item at a time. Appreciate your dishware as you line up each item carefully in the dish rack to air-dry.

Take the PRESSURE OFF

Putting timelines in your life may help you stay on task. However, if you find you are feeling pressured by having to achieve something in a certain order or by a certain deadline, remind yourself that you are enough, just as you are. Your accomplishments may very well be something to strive for, but they by no means measure your worth. You already have everything you need. Setting goals and pursuing your dreams expand who you already are rather than who you hope or wish to be.

PUT YOUR PHONE DOWN

Take a moment to take stock of your technology use. Is there one simple change you could make that would help you be more conscious of how and when you interact with your screens?

Possibilities include:

- Turning off push notifications.
- Using an old-school alarm clock instead of your phone.
- Powering down all your devices at least thirty minutes before bed.
- Deciding on something you'll do before checking your phone, such as taking three breaths or doing ten jumping jacks.

Choose just one tactic you can commit to. You want to set yourself up for success—too many rules may make you feel intimidated and unmotivated.

SHAKE IT OFF

Sometimes when stress or negativity just won't go away, you can get rid of it by literally shaking (or flinging or flailing) it off your body. Physical actions can be a very present and effective way to act out changes you want to make. This is a great, short exercise for shaking off your negativity so you have room to embrace calm.

1. Stand up where you are and feel your feet firmly on the ground.

2. Lift one foot at a time and shake your leg while you inhale and exhale three times for each leg. If balancing is hard for you, hold on to the back of a chair so you don't fall.

3. After you shake out both legs, shake out your arms for three long breaths.

USE

Mala
Beads TO
Meditate

Malas are beads—numbering 108—strung on a loop. This is a sacred number in the yogic tradition. Mala beads are made of various materials, including wood, gemstones, and crystals. As you infuse them with blessings and prayers, your malas will hold that vibration.

1. Get in a comfortable position for meditation in a quiet spot.

2. Choose a mantra. This can be any phrase that has power for you. The most basic mantra is *Om*.

3. Start with the bead next to the "guru" bead, which is the bead at the knot. Hold the first bead between your thumb and middle finger. Move the beads between those two fingers, one by one; at each bead repeat the mantra you've chosen.

4. When you've passed each bead through your fingers and you arrive at the guru bead, you've done 108 repetitions of the mantra. Do not cross over or use the guru bead. Instead, you can do another round by passing the beads between your fingers in the other direction.

5. After you've completed your meditation for the number of rounds you've chosen, stop and integrate the experience. Allow the effects of the meditation to resonate within you.

Enjoy Some Quiet Time

If you always have the TV or the radio on,
or if you always fall asleep to the TV or to music,
then you've probably got a noise habit.

Noise can temporarily mask your loneliness or nervousness.
It can calm an anxious mind or distract a troubled mind.
Constant noise can provide a welcome relief from oneself, but
if it is compromising your ability to think and perform as well as
you could, or if it is keeping you from confronting your stress and
yourself, then it's time to make some space for silence in your life.
Too much noise is stressful on the body and the mind. Give
yourself a break and let yourself experience silence at least
ten minutes each day.

Sculpt WITH Play-Doh

You probably spent more time squeezing and squashing Play-Doh than making sculptures when you were a kid. It smelled funny, but it was magical in its own way.

Now that you're a bit older, you can still have fun molding Play-Doh into jungle animals or flowers, and knead your stress away as you work with the dough. Buy a few jars and create a wonderful sculpture. Or you can make your own dough by combining flour, water, salt, vegetable oil, and a little food dye.

MEDITATE
ON the
SOUNDS
Around You

Modern life is full of stressful, peace-disrupting noise—from the insistent electronic sounds of our computers and smartphones to the beeping of a microwave oven to the roar of traffic on city streets. Rather than try to block out all sound (which is unnatural and can trigger negative episodes), use this meditation to determine how much sound you want to hear, and be able to take the sound in calmly and with pleasure.

1. In your most comfortable meditation posture, close your eyes. Begin to listen.

2. Start with the farthest sounds you can identify. For example, if you hear water running from a faucet down the hallway, listen to it to the exclusion of all else. The goal is to hear only the running faucet and nothing else.

3. Now go to the next sound that presents itself nearer to you. For instance, if you hear the wind blowing against the window of the room you're in, listen to it and exclude everything else.

4. Continue listening to sounds that are ever closer to you. Conclude with the sounds of your breath and your heartbeat.

5. Open your eyes and start again to listen to the sounds of your everyday life.

Take a Walk

No matter where you walk, you can use the time as an opportunity to engage in a walking meditation to create a bit of calm in your day.

Keep in mind that you have no destination, just walking... that's it. Let go of any worries or concerns as you walk. Keep a smile on your face. Slow your walk to a stroll. This is not power walking.

See things as if for the first time, as if you have been blind all of your life and now you can see. Notice all of the beauty that you see, from clouds in the sky to veins in a leaf, and really look at everything, surrendering all judgment. Let go of having to arrive anywhere and simply focus on enjoying the process of walking, surrounded by light and air and beauty. To keep the activity meditative, remember to keep returning your focus to your posture and your breath. Notice how peaceful and quiet your mind has become, and remember this feeling so you can tap back into it when things begin to pick up speed.

Do the
SO HUM CHANT
for PEACE

The So Hum chant is a traditional chant that's meant to reflect the sound of your breath—So: inhale, Hum: exhale.

1. Sit cross-legged with a straight spine and palms resting up and open on your knees. Or sit in any comfortable position you can hold for a little while.

2. Close your eyes and focus your attention on the point between your eyebrows; do not strain.

3. Think the word *So* as you draw the breath in and *Hum* as you breathe out.

4. Keep your mind focused on that spot between your eyebrows (the third eye chakra), and on your breath.

If in our daily life we can smile,
if we can be peaceful and happy,
not only we, but everyone
will profit from it.

THICH NHAT HANH,
Buddhist monk and author

WATCH *your* BREATH

This breath watching will, with even a few minutes, calm the nervous system and bring a feeling of peace. Close your eyes. Close your mouth. Take a few minutes to pay attention to your breath.

1 Notice the length of each inhale.

2 Notice the direction of the breath. When you inhale, can you feel the breath filling your lungs and causing your belly to expand? Can you feel the breath entering your nose and cooling the inside and then passing downward into your lungs?

3 After bringing all this awareness to the breath as it is, slowly begin to inhale longer and deeper. Each inhale should be about five or six seconds long and the exhale should be an equal length of time.

4 Bring your right hand to your belly. Breathe deeply (five or six seconds), drawing in air until your belly presses into your hand. As you exhale, let your navel sink until it is pressing toward your spine.

REMEMBER *That* YOU'RE IN CONTROL

People who are anxious or stressed can often feel trapped by situations in their life. If you're feeling stuck, try this exercise.

Recite the following phrase:

> *Choice is freedom.*
> *I choose to _____.*

In the blank, fill in an empowering statement. For example, rather than saying "I have to go to work," instead say "I choose to go to work." Then add how this choice benefits you: "By going to work, I can afford a nice place to live, good food to eat, and hobbies I enjoy." This phrasing gives you more energy and puts you back in the driver's seat as a cocreator of your life experiences, and helps reassure and calm you when you feel powerless.

Create a Ritual

*You can ward off stress by creating a ritual
that nourishes you and that you do every day,
even if five minutes is all you can find.*

It could be pruning flowers in your garden, enjoying a
glass of lemonade while sitting in your backyard, or going
online to find a recipe you're dying to try. It could be absolutely
anything that pleases you, as long as it reminds you that you
need a little pampering too.

Take a Calming Shower

You can make your shower even more peaceful by making it a mindful shower. Clear your mind of any distractions, and state your intention clearly: "I am shedding all my worries to focus on my body and my senses."

1 Stand still for a few minutes, letting the water run over you, quieting all thoughts, experiencing the rejuvenating powers of warm water.

2 Turn your attention to your feelings. Breathe in relaxation, and breathe out frustration. Notice as worries dissipate and how it feels when muscle tension subsides.

3 Pay attention to your senses: Smell the fragrance in your soap or shampoo, and feel the rough texture of your scrub brush. Allow the smells and textures to conjure up pleasant memories. Listen to the water as it cascades over your head and hair.

4 Toward the end of your shower, take a few really deep breaths, saying *ahhhhhh* as you exhale.

5 Stay focused on sensations as you climb out. Notice the texture of the towel you use to dry yourself. Notice how it absorbs the water, how clean your dry skin feels against the towel.

Do COBRA POSE

Cobra Pose is a great energizing yoga pose for the middle of the day.

1. Stand facing a wall. Place your hands at shoulder height and press them against the wall. Spread your fingers, feeling them press into the wall, and bring your elbows close to your rib cage.

2. Lean forward until your body is pressed against the wall and your forehead is resting on the wall. Take a few breaths with your eyes closed. Inhale and press firmly into your hips. Exhale, lift your heart center as though you want to press it up toward the ceiling.

3. Take a few breaths, and then on the exhale, bring your forehead back to the wall.

Create
YOUR OWN
Sanctuary

As you go along in your busy day, it can seem impossible to find a peaceful moment anywhere. This meditation reminds you that you carry a sanctuary of calm within you wherever you go.

1. Sit up straight with your eyes closed. Begin by breathing deeply, concentrating your awareness between the eyes.

2. Gradually move your center of awareness downward until it rests in the center of your chest. Now begin to see this space. You may sense darkness, or you may visualize your heart and lungs expanding and contracting.

3. Now allow this area to fill with a white light tinged with violet. Picture this light as a countervailing force against the words and images in your head, just as the sun breaks through rain clouds after a storm. Make this inner vision stronger, until the light is extremely powerful.

4. After the visualization is established, stop trying to consciously produce it. Go back to simply observing. Realize that light and darkness are not opposites but part and parcel of the same reality.

Tune Out Drama

Interpersonal drama is created from conflict, insecurity, and pain, and it can be a huge roadblock to a calm and peaceful existence, especially if you get sucked into the fight.

Perhaps you live in a family where gossip and conflict are common. Or maybe your workplace environment is like this. These types of family and/or work dynamics can get quite heated with tension. In an attempt to cope with the situation, you may be forced to detach yourself from it all. This may work to some degree, but tuning out or walking away is only a part of the process. See yourself as becoming neutral to what is happening. This means the drama does not impact you either way. In other words, you are able to observe without being drawn in.

Remember,
the entrance door to the
sanctuary is inside you.

RUMI, Persian philosopher,
theologian, and poet

Walk It Out

Whether you're walking outside your apartment or on your way to a meeting at work, take advantage of any random and precious quiet moments in your day to meditate.

1. As you walk, visualize a question or problem you're stuck on.

2. Imagine it as a labyrinth and think of yourself as walking toward the center.

3. Cultivate gratitude. With each step you take, say "I'm grateful" with sincerity.

4. Focus on taking very slow steps. As thoughts unrelated to your focus come up, let them go.

5. As helpful thoughts come up, express gratitude for them. Continue walking until you have a solution, or until your mind is settled enough for you to sit down and get to business.

LIFT YOUR FACE *to the* SUN

Think about how good you feel after sitting (even briefly) in the sun. If you work or live in a high-pressure or negative environment, consider taking time to go outside for a few minutes a day (particularly if it's sunny). When you do, take a moment to express gratitude to the sun for providing you with light and warmth, and for sharing its energy with you.

COLOR

As a kid you probably spent hours coloring with markers, crayons, and colored pencils. Remember trying really hard to stay inside the lines?

Now that you're a grownup, you can relax and not worry so much about boundaries. Creative activity is a great way to calm your mind and focus your energy. So go out and buy your favorite coloring tools, and since this pastime has become popular with people of all ages, you'll find plenty of coloring books made for adults. Spend the afternoon coloring away; doing it while sprawled out on the living room floor, the way you did when you were little, is always an option.

DO COBBLER'S POSE

A great yoga position for relaxation is called Cobbler's Pose. This pose gets its name from the position that cobblers in India traditionally assumed while they worked. Designed to open the hips and release tension, Cobbler's Pose is a wonderful way to unwind. You can do it anytime, but it's especially effective when done in bed at the end of the day.

1. To begin, lie on your back in bed.

2. Bend your knees, bringing your feet closer to your hips, and then open your knees to the sides. To make the pose more comfortable, you can put a pillow under each knee.

3. You can read a book while in this pose (make sure you have sufficient reading light), or just hold the pose for a few minutes in the dark before you fall asleep.

Do a Metta Meditation

When you focus on loving-kindness toward yourself and others, anxiety and fear will no longer dominate your feelings. This practice is called metta meditation, in which you concentrate your energy on sending compassion to yourself and to other people.

1. Close your eyes; draw your attention inward to your heart center. Picture your tender heart, and say to yourself: "May I be brave and wise and happy." Repeat this a few times in your mind.

2. Next, think of someone you love whose courage and compassion you admire. Picture that person in your mind, and say: "May you be brave and wise and happy."

3. Then picture someone you find challenging or difficult, and address this person in the same way: "May you be brave and wise and happy."

Your sacred space is
where you can find yourself
again and again.

JOSEPH CAMPBELL,
American professor and author

Draw
PEACE
from the
EARTH

You can draw peace and calm from the earth with this simple meditation. Try it while lying on your back on a yoga mat or on a folded blanket on the ground.

1. Lie on your back with a long spine and with your legs straight out and your arms resting at your sides.

2. Release your worries, stress, and tension and give them over to the power of the earth.

3. Breathe in and visualize waves of peaceful energy flowing into your spine and radiating out to all parts of your body.

4. Breathe out, feeling gratitude while visualizing all of that energy soaking back into the earth.

DO A
RED LIGHT

MEDITATION

The next time you're in your car, use each red light as a reminder to take one full breath that you pay attention to the whole way through. Stop. Inhale. Exhale. How does it change your experience of your commute? Do you notice any difference in how you feel once you get out of the car and go on with your day? Finding quiet times in the day to remember to breathe can help you keep a calm, peaceful energy all day long.

Take a Yoga Class

Yoga classes come in many different flavors:
Some are restorative, while
some are created to make you sweat.

But all of them help you strengthen your connection to your body and to your energy, which is so important to keeping your reserve of inner calm. You shouldn't be intimidated by yoga—you can start slow, improve your technique as you stretch and strengthen your muscles, and learn the proper feel of all the poses. Don't be too eager to achieve the "perfect" pose and correct bad posture habits immediately. It took a lifetime to get you where you are today. One yoga class won't change all that. In yoga, being present to each moment along the journey is more important than the destination—and it's also a lot more interesting!

PERFORM THE
Simplest Meditation

Meditation is about focusing your mind and concentrating on your breath. You can meditate anywhere at any time, especially if you keep it simple.

Try this simple meditation to calm your mind when you're feeling stressed. All you have to do is follow the breath and anchor it to a word or phrase.

1. Inhale and say silently to yourself: "**PEACE**."
2. Exhale and say silently to yourself: "**RELAX**."

Inhale...Peace. Exhale...Relax. Have no agenda—just the breath. This seems almost too simple, but the results can be significant in terms of releasing stress, slowing down, and centering yourself.

LIE IN
Savasana

A nap in the yoga pose Savasana can remind you to be mindful as you relax and refresh yourself.

1. Bring your arms straight down by your sides. If you are cold, bring your arms close to your body, and if you are warm, move your hands about several inches or more away from your sides. You can cover yourself with a soft blanket if you'd like.

2. When you feel rested (or when your music or timer cues you that the time is over), roll to your side, come up slowly, pause to take a few deep, cleansing breaths, and then open your eyes.

Smile,
breathe, and
go slowly.

THICH NHAT HANH,
Buddhist monk and author

Find Your Breathing Space

Where is your breathing space? Where do you feel most at ease? What time of day is most peaceful to you? Think about where and when you can take a minute, away from all distractions, and breathe.

If you don't have a designated space already, look for one that you can start training your brain to associate with calm. Consider taking a moment to roam outside. Be curious about the breathing spaces around you. Perhaps you'll notice a tree, your front porch step, or a certain pathway. A breathing space can also be a special area in your home where you can limit distractions (like TV noise, phone alerts, new emails, or interruptions from family members). Such a space might be a quiet corner of your bedroom, a path outside, a certain chair or spot at the kitchen table where you see the birds clearly through a window, or anywhere else you can go to find a moment to breathe. Make time to spend at least a few minutes in your breathing space every day.

TAKE *a* NAP

*If your last nap was twenty to thirty years ago,
take some time today for a quick nap.*

A quick thirty-minute midday nap has been proven to
lessen stress, increase learning, and improve health. This
may be hard if you are at work, but even closing your eyes
for five minutes in your office is proven to relieve stress
and give you a boost of energy. Those few moments will
help you decompress and give your body the needed break
it deserves. Be careful of napping for more than an hour, as
you may have a hard time falling asleep that evening.

Stomp!

Stomping your feet is a great way to ground your energy and create a feeling of calm and stability. If you feel like you're carrying around a lot of negative, stressed-out energy, stomp it off! If you stomp outside, you leave the energy out there.

Let it go.

You can even stomp your feet outside each day after work before entering your home.

PICK UP A TEXTILE CRAFT

The rhythm of clacking needles, the feel of soft yarn between your fingers, the persistent lull of the contiguous stitches, and the gentle pop as the needle pokes through the fabric—these are the sensuous pleasures of knitting, crocheting, cross-stitch, and other textile crafts that create space in your life to allow enlightenment to happen. The repetitive actions and soothing rhythms help you take a break from thinking and worrying, and let you focus on the mechanics of your activity. You can learn these crafts with the help of a friend, a class, or online videos. The best part is that once you're done with your crafting meditation, you'll have a beautiful finished product to keep or to give away as a lovely, mindful gift.

Set an Intention

An intention is like a force field that you set around your thoughts—giving you a focus that keeps your mind from spinning in multiple directions.

To set one for yourself, create a simple statement about how you want to be (don't get too attached to a specific result, or else your subconscious may not buy it). Here are some examples of intentions you may want to set for yourself:

Today, I'll stay curious when I get challenged.

I'll look for the good in every situation.

I'll find opportunities to do good.

Whenever things get stressful,
I'll have a safe harbor to return to.

TAKE A BREATHER

The life-force or living energy connects to all that there is and sustains our life breath.

The following exercise helps open up your life-force passages. Focusing on your breath can allow you to let go of anxieties and fears that are keeping your breath shallow. It helps you physically release tension, and gives you a mental focal point for keeping yourself calm.

1 Sit upright with your spine straight.

2 Open your mouth, relax your jaw, stick out your tongue, and pant like a dog.

3 Continue for several minutes. These in-and-out breaths will open up your belly and clear the energy passageways from the base of your spine to your throat's vocal cords.

Be like a river.
Be ever present
and flowing.

GURMUKH KAUR KHALSA,
American yoga teacher

Index

INVITE HAPPINESS INTO YOUR LIFE!

PICK UP OR DOWNLOAD YOUR COPY TODAY!